The Family Book of Martyrs

Benjamin Myers

The Family Book of Martyrs

Benjamin Myers

LITERARY PRESS
LAMAR UNIVERSITY

ISBN: 978-1-942956-97-6
LOC:

Lamar University Literary Press
Beaumont, TX

To my sisters

Recent Poetry from Lamar University Literary Press

Lisa Adams, *Xuai*
Walter Bargen, *My Other Mother's Red Mercedes*
Christine Boldt, *In Every Tatter*
Devan Burton, *A Room for Us*
Jerry Bradley, *Collapsing into Possibility*
Mark Busby, *Through Our Times*
Julie Chappell, *Mad Habits of a Life*
Stan Crawford, *Resisting Gravity*
Glover Davis, *Academy of Dreams*
William Virgil Davis, *The Bones Poems*
Chris Ellery, *Elder Tree*
Dede Fox, *On Wings of Silence*
Alan Gann, *That's Entertainment*
Larry Griffin, *Cedar Plums*
Michelle Hartman, *Irony and Irrelevance*
Katherine Hoerth, *Goddess Wears Cowboy Boots*
Lynn Hoggard, *First Light*
Michael Jennings, *Crossings: A Record of Travel*
Gretchen Johnson, *A Trip Through Downer, Minnesota*
Markham Johnson, *Dear Dreamland*
Betsy Joseph & Chip Dameron, *Relatively Speaking*
Ulf Kirchdorfer, *Chewing Green Leaves*
Jim McGarrah, *A Balancing Act*
J. Pittman McGehee, *Nod of Knowing*
Laurence Musgrove, *Bluebonnet Sutras*
Benjamin Myers, *Black Sunday*
Janice Northerns, *Some Electric Hum*
Godspower Oboido, *Wandering Feet on Pebbled Shores*
Carol Coffee Reposa, *Sailing West*
Jan Seale, *Particulars*
Steven Schroeder, *the moon, not the finger, pointing*
Glen Sorestad, *Hazards of Eden*
Vincent Spina, *The Sumptuous Hills of Gulfport*
W.K. Stratton, *Betrayal Creek*
Wally Swist, *Invocation*
Ken Waldman, *Sports Page*
Loretta Diane Walker, *Ode to My Mother's Voice*
Dan Williams, *At the Gates, a Refuge of Milkweed and Sunflowers*
Jonas Zdanys, *The Angled Road*

For information on these and other Lamar University Literary
Press books go to www.Lamar.edu/literarypress

Acknowledgements

I would like to thank the editors of the following publications, where some of the poems in this manuscript were previously published:

Arcadia
Books and Culture
The Christian Century
Cimarron Review
Concho River Review
Dragon Poet Review
Ekstasis
First Things
Image
Ink & Letters
Mid/South Anthology
Measure
Modern Age
Ninth Letter
Oklahoma Humanities
Oklahoma Today
Poetry Northwest
Raintown Review
Ragazine
The Red Earth Review
The Red River Review
Redivider
Relief
Rock & Sling
Saint Katherine Review
The Same
The Texas Review
Trinity House Review
San Pedro River Review
Story South
This Land Press
Tupelo Quarterly
Windhover
The Yale Review

CONTENTS

I. Martyrs and Orphans

The Orphans

My children are pretending that I'm dead.
The spider leaves of the mimosa tree
for shade, they play a game they call "the orphans,"
stretched out in grass bald dirt beside the roots
and moaning as they wake from some imagined
airplane crash that has left them all alone
in darkest jungle. Right away they start
to gather leaves and drop them in a bucket
full of rain water, stirring with a stick
and calling it breakfast. I sit on the porch
and think, *What level-headed kids we've raised,*
attending to the most important meal
even with my charred and smoking corpse nearby!
But then I think of my own mother standing
at our screen door, already in her fifties when
her mother died but bawling out
into the fields, *I am an orphan,*
like she was giving voice to something we
all know. The children tiptoe out from shade,
into the glare of sun, exploring
their jungle home. They are rehearsing worst
scenarios but also drawing lines
around themselves, like people
in their coloring books contoured in solid black
for filling in later. The cat with a lazy eye
is watching them. They've put mimosa blossoms
in their hair. Sitting on the porch, I float
between the generations and hear
the children's voices tearing ragged strips
from summer quiet. I stand, wanting to call
to them out there in all that heavy light,
but I can barely see them now in the glare.
And when I raise my hand to block the sun,
I freeze, suddenly aware of how much
I look like a man who is waving goodbye.

Elizabeth Discovers Rock and Roll

Arms angled, thin and small, waving
above her head, my five-year-old
daughter is dancing like a maenad
in the morning light of the white
tiled bathroom. An old clock-radio
in a windowsill up high coughs
out a.m. oldies, while I bathe
her little brother. She is slapping
the cold tile with her bare toes, swirling
the bathmat as she twirls beside the toilet.

Her great grandparents danced
this freely at house dances
in Oklahoma in the thirties,
heavy furniture pushed back
against the walls, rugs rolled up.
They swung each other across wooden
floor like a carnival ride while outside
men passed a jug of something fiery sweet
in the moon-shadow of the farmhouse, listened
while fiddles and guitars thrummed fingers
against the black edges of night.

Now their descendent dances
between the pedestal sinks,
knocking the towel
from its hanging ring
while the Big Bopper sings
"Chantilly Lace."

Later I will switch off the radio
when a report comes on about a man
in Texas who has barricaded himself
and his young son into their home
and set the whole thing on fire,
because this is not the morning
she discovers the long burning
fuse of alcoholism that snakes
sizzling into her genes,
or the rages and sulks
that soak and chafe

her ancestral heart.
This is not the morning she finds out
how we have counted the things
of this world by putting one bullet in each.

The light stumbles in
through the blinds,
spills itself on the white tile
floor, where Elizabeth dances
like David before the lord,
her last baby fat bouncing
in a slight paunch
above her thin legs.
A school bus rumbles past
outside the window.
The morning tilts itself
toward eight o'clock,

and I am praying now,
my daughter, for you:
eyes to see even in the weight
of darkness around us
and feet to move all
the way through it.

My Daughter Asks about some Bombs in Europe

I don't know what I am supposed to say,
the TV barking on its chain all day:
the black ski-masks, guns, bombs enough to blow
a block apart. The news reporters show
the piles of rubble raked in stacks like hay.

At bedtime, through debris, I pick my way—
the toys, books, clothes left on the floor from play—
and think, *How to explain*? Maybe you know;
I don't. "Know what?"

my daughter says, "I think I want to stay
with you forever." *You will go away
and should,* I think but hope the going will be slow.
When she's asleep, I'll close the book and go
back to my room, drop knees to rug and pray
I don't know what.

The Cat in the Cistern

This house so old it keeps stone stomachs down
beside the basement underneath the porch:
three cisterns holding water long forgotten,
sealed tight with concrete caps, until one cracks,
crumbles a bit, enough to let a stray
cat slip through, fall in. Two days we hear
it bawl an echoing bawl, but we can't find
the source at first. Then, crawling on my gut
beneath the porch, I follow the small sound
and shoot a flashlight through the narrow crack,
see eyes flash back a dark twenty or more
feet down: the kitten, wet and sitting on
a little bit of stone jutting from wall
above dark water. We begin to try
to get it out: can't crack the concrete more,
afraid the falling rock will kill the cat;
can't get the cat to grab a dangled rope.
I hunt through hardware stores for something long
enough and looped for grabbing but find nothing
right. Animal control won't come. The cat
gets weaker, tries less hard to clutch the things
we lower down to it, and giving up
begins to loom ahead like a grain silo seen
a long way down a Kansas highway stretch.
Two more days spent trying to get the cat
to snatch the volleyball net we lowered
into the hole, and then we quit. We turn
the music up so that the kids can't hear
the mewlings float like lost balloons by one
or two from down below the sagging porch.
I cannot save them all, the things that want
me to. Turn up the Mozart more, until
the bawling stops. And when it does it will
not be the same silence with which we started.

The Fall

Like a water stain grows on old carpet,
a bruise is spreading on my daughter's cheek
after she's fallen from the hanging rings
at her gymnastics class. Girls in pink tights—
one inexplicable in a tutu—flock around her
on the mat over which they've one by one been rising
above the smell of sweaty feet and chalk
to hang a breathless moment and dismount.

Later we cruise the supra lighted aisles
for milk and bread, the bruise now screaming blue
across her face. The other shoppers eye
us like suspicious fruit. I did not hit
my daughter. I most likely wouldn't think
they think I had if my teeth were straighter,
my clothes not off the discount rack. Wheeling
my girl past canned goods, I remember the woman
in dark brown corduroy and brown floral blouse,
who followed the cart my mother pushed me in
through this same store to ask and ask
about my busted nose and swollen eye,
not taking the grownup's word for it—
my sister had thrown a toy truck—
but directing the repeated question to me:
how did you get hurt, little boy?
My mother could be loud, as can I,
but never hit me.
In the checkout line,
my daughter eyes the candy rack, touches
her face and then recoils, wincing.
The cashier keeps one eye on her. Will she
call DHS? I don't know why I feel
guilty. I never hit my girl. I drop a bag
of little gummy fish in fruity colors
onto the running belt beside the clerk,
pull out my wallet, show that I can pay.

Martyrologue #1

Felecia loved the bright wood-paneled room
in which her class met at St. Genevieve
School, and her teachers loved to watch her 'bloom.'
But when tuition rose, she had to leave.
Despite the fact that at the public school
they made her sit beside a boy who ate
erasers while he leaked a pinkish drool,
she never said a word about her fate.
But long years later when her aging father asks,
the paper flattened on his lap and folded twice,
What is a seven letter word that starts
with C and means a group that gives advice?
She shrugs and says with tone that's Kansas-flat,
Now where would I have learned a thing like that?

After the Ice Storm

A thaw begins and falling ice descends
suddenly from three pecan trees

by our drive. Inside, behind me,
a girl practices piano, her descending

scales a part of the whole world that is
falling. The limbs crack and groan

with the broken joy of a man stretching himself
after long confinement. Yesterday, the power

went off for five hours and I wanted to like it—
imagined the family flocked by the wood stove,

life peeled back to its solid pit—
but the whole cold dark time I

walked through the house flipping
dead light switches, lifting

spaces between the slats of blinds
to watch for blinking lights

on utility trucks. I am always
worried about my children.

Sunlight bounces blindly between the chunks
of ice on their way down. The descending scales

stumble and stop. It would be dangerous to walk down
the steps and out beneath the trees. Still, I want

to step into that world of gravity and glass,
to stand beneath the stinging shards and listen

to the shattering, keeping count as everything
that's going to be broken goes ahead and gets broken

already.

Martyrologue #2

I know a gifted man who left the stage,
because, he said, his kids can't eat his dreams.
And yet they did, he adds with a sighing laugh.
He moved the family back to Tulsa
and sells boat insurance from a metal desk
behind a plate glass window in a strip
mall where the nail salon next door fills up
his nose and head with fumes. He rarely thinks
about the roles he might have played, except for when
an empty beer can blows across the parking lot
and makes a clatter almost like applause.

Decoration Day

We slice thick circles of bologna, lay
them on white bread beside the tilting grave
stones, to picnic with the dead. Beyond the fence
a mountain dams back open field where steers
drink muddy pond. We've come to pin down wreaths
of paper flowers, brought our old toothbrushes
to scrub the grooves that spell our lost ones' names.

This holiday was started for the rebel dead,
but now we come to clean the graves of all
our folk. In cemeteries through these hills
the Weed Eaters are whipping at pale stones
to clear the dandelion, henbit, poke
and years. There's not enough remembering
still.
          Now my 7-year-old daughter climbs
the low and lonely tree grown here and sits
against the light in thin top branches so
that when she calls I have to reach into
the sun to lift her down. I show her where
her people's graves lean each way out in line.
She tries to read the names. I try to teach
her. Family women stoop and touch the stones
with cleaning cloths, as gentle as the first
women some long millennia ago
to stoop and touch the rangy dogs that slinked
beyond the circled huts. I think these are
the rituals we've always used to tame
a wild, panting animal like grief.

Listening to Reggae at the Nashville Airport

A nitpicky and nagging little rain berates the tarmac
window where travelers float by, pale
in reflection, not like the departing
souls we call ghosts; more like souls failing
to come fully into being at all.

Riding the redeye Nashville to Oklahoma City,
I'm bound to be in the company of more than one
failed Garth Brooks. I have fallen into a gray
vinyl chair at Gate B4, where, looking around,
I see misanthropy is the sin that so easily besets me.
The bouncy sounds of Bob Marley
roll through a pipe into the artificial terminal light,
odd choice for Nashville and a rainy late-night Sunday.

A little while and the rain is chiding faster.
I'm thinking now about last week, when two friends
expecting their first baby showed me the nursery
décor: little cartoon arks struck against a sea of blue
wallpaper, each ark of a hundred sprouting dopey
giraffe eyes on a neck through a window, each ark
with a dove sitting like a weathervane on top.

I guess they want baby to know about the time God
killed just about everybody. This is a foam
churning world with a wild God.
The introduction is apt.
Sometimes I understand God's impulse.

For instance, these Gate B4 people, Jesus,
help me not to hate them, their oversized cowboy
hats like dark owls or albino possums on their heads,
jeans be-glittered across the ass with crosses.
My mean thoughts are like a ball
some kid keeps bouncing
against a wall of the house where they lay out the dead.

When I was a boy, my father showed me once an arrowhead,
flinty and flat in his dirty palm. "Where is the Indian,"
I said. "He's dead." "Who killed him,"
I said. "I think we did." And I knew

24

for the first time the cold, wet weight of the world's
sorrow and, at the same time, my small part in it.

And now an airport full of dollar store cowboys
and a rolling Rastafarian vibe and all of us,
somehow together, about to careen
madly through the spitting, hissing dark
until we, like a wild turkey fat with foraged grain, just barely
lift off the ground.

Martyrologue #3

For fifty years he won't forget the dew
that wet his denim cuffs through to his socks
those early August mornings when he rose
into the thinning dark to milk the cows.
His younger brother rasped in heavy sleep,
still snugly bunked beneath a thin patched quilt:
hard to resist resentment, even with
the asthma blooming like a summer storm-
cloud in his younger brother's chest. No rest
for the first born. He'd trudge through wettened grass,
the sleep still smearing trees into the sky
seen through the corners of his eyes. Long years
later he'll stand beside his brother's grave,
the dew just burning off the fresh cut grass
as mourners trickle back into their cars,
and on the wind that tumbles through the stones
he'll catch the scent of cow dung and fresh cream.

The Family Book of Martyrs

Not the red leather bound and weighty tome,
its gothic letters sharp as raven's beak,
that sat unread in your grandmother's home,
fat as a Borgia pope in holy week.

I mean instead the unseen book or scroll
that tells the sacrifice of every mom,
dad, brother, sister; that records the toll
of love and labor met with great aplomb

or not, but met. For instance, take the time
you had the lead in your school play, rehearsed
for weeks but then as you prepared to climb
the stage, your sister's dumb appendix burst

and no one in your family saw the show.
Or call to mind the hours your mother spent
with bleach and wax to make the flooring glow
before you tracked in mud and ruined it.

We ink in what we gave and what we took;
we illustrate the wounds and petty slights.
Then back and forth we pass the ragged book
to read aloud through threadbare winter nights.

Voyager

A boy rides in circles on his trike
inside the yellow light of an open garage.
Driving home after dark, I see him there,
a little spinning world, all self-contained.

I know the family, know his mother must,
though unseen, be somewhere nearby watching,
but in that skinny light he seems so all
alone. Childhood is very lonely, I think

and look into the rearview mirror, where
the oldest of my three kids sits in back
and reads by flashlight while I drive her home.
Each time she turns the page, a shadow moves

across her face. I know, despite my books
on fathering, she travels milky space capsuled
in her own thoughts. I know I hold her
only in an ever looser orbit.

II. Historical Markers

Night Hoops

With tar still sludging our fingers from roofing
jobs worked through the heat of day, with scratches
down our forearms from cutting brush,
with sunburned backs, poison ivy riding
our sore calves, behind the old legion
hut, around a pole over a patch
of cracked concrete illuminated
by one leaning lamppost and an August
moon twenty years ago: hoops.

Far from city ball, if we dribbled too far the bounce
smothered in gravel and dirt, but we kept
close to the pole and counted anything off
the concrete as three.

Tonight I'm watching basketball on TV
with the sound turned down, and hear instead the rubber
pounding into baked concrete beneath
the broken windows of the abandoned hut,
June bugs bouncing off the yellow light.
I let my eyes fall shut and see us jostling,
bumping, reaching across to steal
the ball, breaking for the basket, battling
over limited territory.

We played because we had nowhere else
to be or because work had worn us
to bare sleeplessness. Or we played to stay gone
until an empty bottle dropped from someone's
half-dead hand.

And from this distance I know what
is going to happen: one of us will go
to war and return with an empty sleeve.
Another will lose a child and grieve tearlessly,
his whole life an eroding city under a coarse
cloud of dust . The rest of us will drift
off to jobs or jail, off to divorces
and the rusty nail of small humiliations, moving
apart as silently and subtly as sluggish continents.

Looking back now, I see us there pushing, posting
up, tugging on sweaty t-shirts,
and I don't know if we are attempting to keep
each other away from the basket
or desperately trying to hold one another inside
that thin circle of light.

My Grandfather's Fake Rolex

The one the pawnbroker rubbed his stubby thumb
over to show me how gold plating flakes from fakes.
The one I couldn't get enough for to buy a case of beer so kept
in a Chinese teapot on my bookshelf for years,
a fitting inheritance from a man whose fake hair
used to make me laugh in secret,
who talked about his bombing missions in the war
but never mentioned they were training missions
over Nebraska. A fitting inheritance for
a man who once told a colleague he played
high school football, even though I quit
after the eighth grade.

We say many things out of the urge
to revise. My father's sister, who bought
her father the watch in Tokyo thirty years after
the war while the cherry blossoms rioted
pink in the streets, could sometimes say
she had a happy childhood
and not mention the mother who abandoned them.

I remember the watch loose
in the pawnbroker's fingers, the way
he turned it like falling
water through his hands,
like water falling and gone.

My Father on the Diving Board

His body browned from working in a heat
that blistered paint and cooked the summer grass
to needle sharp, my father climbed the rungs
of wet metal up to the fiberglass

cat's tongue above the public swimming pool.
Chlorine singed my nose, dyed my sisters' hair
from blond to seasick green, and horseflies bit
us as they swarmed the heat-thinned humid air.

But it was worth it all to see my father
dive. He, before the cancer wormed its way
out of his menthol smokes into his lungs,
pushed a shovel all week. Then Saturday

he'd swim. He slowly backed until the board
dipped low and bowed up in the middle, then,
from toes tensed taut as ten piano strings,
the sun tan oil gleaming on his skin,

flipped like a silver dollar in the air,
and plunged into the cooling cavity
to show how even weightless grace depends
on the unflinching force of gravity.

Mr. Goodbody

We sat Indian style on the spotted carpet
of the little library, me and the other children
from One Horse, Oklahoma, where half
the kids were Indians, although I don't know how
they sat at home. The teacher wheeled
in a big TV strapped to a cart,
like a buffalo on a gurney.
There, on the screen, Slim Goodbody danced
without his skin. His lungs, his liver, all
his innards there for us to see.
The girls squirmed, and the boys laughed.
One asked, *where'd his balls go to*.
But I thought, *there* I am: open
before the world, painfully sensitive
to touch, heart beating in front of everybody.
Oh, Ich bin ein Slim Goodbody!

Later, I read about the martyrdom
of St. Bartholomew, who was flayed
alive by the pagan king of Armenia.
The picture by his story showed a man
thinly draped around his red sinewy
shoulders with his own limp skin, one foot
dangling over his raw chest like the tassels
of a prayer shawl.

But not until a girl called me a troglobite—
which I had to look up to learn evolved
to transparency from a million years
in lightless depths of caves—did I at last
understand myself: translucent exoskeleton
revealing everything inside, as exposed
and fully legible as anything
coming to be in the dark.

Slide Rule

Scabbarded in red leather, it was a gift
from the bachelor uncle who tutored
me in math, wood smooth, glossy
blonde with worn spots from thumb
and forefinger: as antique
to me as his coins pressed with the profile
of Edward III, or his Bavarian stamps
interred behind glass.

As antique as he, himself, in dark
orthopedic shoes and a thin,
black necktie halfway down his belly
as he sat on his porch swing
with a pellet gun taking pops
at neighborhood dogs who crapped
on his lawn, reading Seneca
and Zane Gray between shots.

I never got far in algebra or geometry,
despite long afternoons with the two
of us bent over his kitchen table, September
sun falling in through the transom,
traffic slurring outside, his whole house
a battleship out to sea and at war
with rushing time.

And I never learned to use the slide rule,
but when he died, I took it from the scabbard,
matched my fingers to places worn by his own
young hands, and studied the numbers
as they glided past like passengers
lined neatly in the windows
of a departing train.

My Grandfather's Workshop

A layer of dust grown thick as winter wool
fleeced hammers, saws, and levels on the shelf
so that each time I lifted some old tool
it left a shaved-in outline of itself.

Inside the old man shook his coffee cup
in speckled hands turned I.V. bruised and weak
that knew once every tool and took them up
as native tongues take up their words to speak.

And in the shop a coffee can of nails
sat shelved as if its death-head's rusty grin
would say *here's how the age of god-men fails:*
thin knees, thin heart, your reign must now begin.

Tornado Warning, 1980

Like men about to fight with knives, the clouds
get low and slowly circle each other

at dusk. The TV weathermen begin
to jump and yell like carnival barkers.

With wives and children closed in cellars, men
go stand on patchy grass and gravel drives

to look the whiskey-violent sky in the eye.
When the tornado drops it wraps itself in rain

and staggers toward the little row of houses.
And still the fathers stand, like matinee

heroes who've bent their ear to the Mojave floor
then straightened up again to look

into the distance for a cloud of dust.
Grown men with families and jobs,

with mortgages on houses in the line
of this swaggering mad and hostile wind,

they cling to what they know of dignity
by standing in the presence of the storm.

And I can see them still and smell the smoke
their Kools and Camels gave up to the wind

that always came for them, that always turned
somewhere beyond the darkened line of trees.

One Horse, OK, pop. 1,000: Saaaaaaalute

Driving home tonight, I see
Loretta Lynn on a casino
billboard and take a left
turn to 1982,
where I find myself sitting
on a red braided rug
in front of the console Zenith
watching *Hee Haw*. Men
in overalls pop up
from cornfields, like ghosts from stony
ground, while girls with shirts tied
below their bubbled breasts giggle.
My father is somewhere working,
his back turning ever deeper
shades of red as he bends to earth
beneath the Oklahoma sun.
My grandma is bedridden
and in love with Johnny Cash,
who she says is a good Baptist.
During commercials he sells bibles,
bound in black, so I believe it.
Outside a pumpjack chugs into the haze,
and a dog whines through the screen door.
There is a block of govt. cheese
next to great grandma's bone-
white gravy bowl on the kitchen table.
When Roy plays banjo, his fingers
jump like fleas off a drowning dog.
My mother has gone
down the gravel road that snores
when trucks dust by, to Walmart,
where she puts our school clothes
on lay-away again.
I stay with Nana.
We take care of each other
and enjoy laughing
at the dumb hicks on T.V.

Word Problem

A man starts walking east onboard
a train that's moving slowly west,
passing through lighted cars at dusk.

Each dimly glowing car
is equal to one year.

How long until the walking man
arrives back at the house he knew
when he was small, the house he could

walk through with all the lights turned off
and still not bump a thing, the house
he could walk through while he's asleep

and often does?

Quail Hunt, One Horse, OK, 1982

The Johnson grass is like a yellow flame
beneath a thin glass dome. My grandfather
this morning wades into that fire,
his 20-gauge draped open in the crook
of his elbow, like a bird he's already shot.
I follow his orange plaid hunting jacket
through waist-high blades of scouring, blonded grass
to pet the dog he's brought for nosing up
the birds from bare and brushy upwards rush
of scrub. I know by the time we cross
this frozen creek again the shells he's spent
will bulge my pocket like a bullfrog's throat.
This man was born before this land was a state
and now begins to knee his way into
the high grass of his last ten years, not yet
frail, not yet waning down to elbow
and kneecap on a hospice bed, still strong
as cedar root in hard red earth. The dog
noses a sudden flash of bobwhites up,
like a handful of dirt clods flung
against the cold clear dome of pre-snow sky.
And some may say to shoot them down is brutal,
but I already know that, in a place
that's mostly sky, to shoot a bird back down
to earth is just a way to keep the rest
of all we've got from rising to follow
and falling up toward that dead-cold,
forever distant, cracked and bluish dome.

Storm Cellar

A rotting wooden door thrown on the cellar floor
above a quarter inch of standing water kept

our shoes dry while we sat on two old rusted cots.
I learned early how to distrust a certain shade

of dirty gold in early summer afternoon
light, knowing it would lead to evening storms and hours

of squatting refuge in the dark and dirty hole.
I tried to read my comics by flashlight. My father

stood in the yard above to watch wall clouds. A near
orphan himself, he was just learning how to save

the objects of his love by shoving them beneath
the ground before the gusting howl could rake its teeth

across the knobby scalps of scrub oaks and red cedars.
He'd leave his patch of gravel every fifteen minutes,

appearing in the square of light atop the cellar stairs
waving as if in some strange form of benediction,

as if to paint a cross of lamb's blood on the lintel.

Benediction, 1982

A motorcycle, ticking as it cools,
pants hot breath on the gravel in the drive
outside our house. It's all chrome and jet black
and has a dragon painted on its shiny tank,
a scaly tail entwined around a girl
who wears a fur bikini: perhaps the greatest piece
of art I've seen in life thus far. The bike
is not my father's bike; he drives a truck
like every dad I know. The man who owns
the bike is bearded, dusty, and denimed
and talking to my father, who then gets on
the thing and rides it down the street in front
of our old house, gunning the engine to scare
the sleepy crows from off the power lines
before he turns around and churns the bricks
back toward the house. Our dog,
an aging collie, runs the length of backyard fence
to bark and jump her pure and trembling joy.

When dad gets back, they squat behind the bike
to light their cigarettes out of the wind.
The bearded man is telling how he'll ride
it all the way out west and camp beside the road
along the way. "You could come too," he says,
"if you could get a bike." My father shakes
his head, steps on his half-smoked cigarette,
and squints into the sun to look him in the eye.
A handshake, then we watch the bearded man
ride off across the 9th street bridge.

When Dad comes back into the house, I know
his coming back is covenant and type
of all the other times he will come home.
I know then too that love is near to sacrifice.
Beside the door he rests his hand
on top of my young head: benediction
implied both in the resting hand and in
the heavy sigh with which he shuts the door.

Culvert

It's corrugated gray like rings of muscle made
for swallowing reminded me of a throat,
that drainage pipe that ran beneath our street.

When playground wars bled into the afternoon,
we were tunnel rats, imagining ourselves
the younger uncles and older cousins back
not long ago from Vietnam. Grasshoppers
as big as clothespins took off from tall weeds
like choppers from the Mekong Delta.

On TV Ollie North murmured his pledge
into a cluster of blank microphones,
his face handsome as varnished wood. Our wars
outside subsided when we found a brief-
case sitting on the dark green stain that smeared
the bottom of the pipe. We knew it was
drug money. We all watched *Miami Vice*.

All that fall my father painted houses
for cash, and I spent Saturdays
scraping flakes of old paint from neighborhood
clapboards, watching curls of faded color
fall across my sunburned hand and land
in the grass around cracked foundations.
We could have used a briefcase full of money.

Prying at the locked case with dirty fingers,
we heard a bang, scrabbled
backwards up the gravel bank, running
scattershot back to our little rooms
at the rear of little, ramshackle houses,
sure that someone was shooting at us.

We didn't go back to the culvert
for weeks, but that night and many
to follow, I dreamed about that briefcase,
thin and brown with a row of rolling gold
numbers for a lock on top, the kind
of thing any of our fathers might
have carried to work, if they'd ever
had that kind of job.

Luminaries

A night one summer otherwise a blank,
somewhere back in the deepest cavity
of youth, a woman on our block poured sand
into twelve paper sacks and dropped a short
fat candle into each to make the walk
to her front porch a warmly glowing path
for dinner guests. This was the 70's.
The adults came and went in their high mystery
of polyester and of sexual love,
their ankles passing inches from those paper bags,
just inches from those flames. In our front yard,
I watched my father pace and fret she'd burn
the whole block down.

                     And now today the trees
 in their October coats glow with the late
afternoon sun behind them, like those paper bags.
And I'm still peering out from the front lawn,
still learning how to live in a world aglow,
a world so brightly close to combustion.

Old Chevy in the Woods

The bench seat grew tufts of stuffing like hair
where the vinyl was ripped. It had three flat tires

and one wheel missing altogether; must have been a 56
or 57, once the color of fresh cream, now pinked

by Oklahoma dust. One more piece of junk
to join the rubble that freaked the woods

near our house: the rusted refrigerators lying
on their backs, gaped mouth to rain;

rolls of chicken wire; Lay-Z Boys
with broken springs; dead window units.

We were fourteen and took turns sitting
behind the steering wheel so worn

it seemed still to shine with the sweat
and grease of an owner dead for all

we knew. We smoked stolen cigarettes,
looked out the broken windows,

already certain that there was nothing
we haven't made

less.

&

I knew a girl who with her tongue could tie
a heart from a cherry stem, but to me they always looked
like ampersands (so I gave her cherries
& cherries & cherries) & I loved her

all that year & into the fall. Mistletoe
clung like mad to the naked branches.
She wore sweaters that left
little white patches of her skin

showing through. What could I do?
Like all the people she had,
I left her too, at the Christmas parade
while the band was marching past,

tubas and trombones igniting
in the disinterested December sun.
& when she was gone,
there on the sidewalk where she was standing,

a cherry stem tied up like an ampersand,
stuck to the concrete & as misshapen
as any actual human heart.

'I am not Prince Hamlet'

At eighteen I had the body of a Greek
philosopher. Skinny as a streetlight,
too slight for football, slow for hoops, I joined
the drama club to meet new girls to be
ignored by, and I found myself standing
slightly to the side on an old wooden stage,
a grease pen mustache smearing my upper lip.
I played the wacky uncle, the sidekick,
the fool and specialized in pratfalls
that really hurt.

        My only friend was a kid
who spent his days recording everything
on HBO onto black VHS
cassettes, archiving them on metal shelves
in his room: *Terminator, Predator,*
and *Kindergarten Cop.* I'd drop
by after school and read the labels.

I felt like a screen door, something
anyone could see through, if they
squinted at it.

        My senior year we played
a melodrama for a dinner theater,
the audience chewing over paper plates
of spaghetti. I played the messenger,
a pony express rider with a bad
stutter, a cheap gag but still better
than the garlic bread. I came on at the end
after the big chinned boy knocked the villain
to the ground, so I could say *the bank has lost
the note. The debt is gone. All is, all is
all all all is well. All is well.*

Historical Markers

My father stopped at every one of them,
a need to know that drove us nuts and slowed
our progress toward the lake. We stood in sweat,
lurking like hitchers by the asphalt road.

The Battle of the Washita; the birth
place of Will Rogers; any church or shoot-
out that one might say mattered stopped us cold
beside the crumbling shoulder of old Route

66. So I'd drag my teenage self
out of the car to nudge the shoulder rocks
with white-toed Converse tips and stand there half
enthused while trying to look bored. Those talks

about the past beside the highway strip
are past now too, my father gone, the darker
years since a road I drive as it gets late,
squinting into the dusk to find a marker.

"Earth's the Place for Love"

The post office still squats, federal and brick,
a toad in a colonial wig, one block
off Main. By night the armadillos dig
for grubs on the respectable lawns
of bespectacled turn-of-the-American-
century homes. And I'm still here, walking
the aisles of the hardware store where round-
end eyes of hanging wrenches watch me pass,
or I'm in the barber shop where my grandfather
had his hair cut close and blocked across the back
of his neck like a taut fence line. The diesel trucks
grumble and thump through town. The little birds
wing in and out of storefront awnings. This morning
I watched a caterpillar make its way
across our concrete drive, playing the squeeze
box of its own green length, and thought
"Hey, little caterpillar, why can't you
get your shit together?" No one wants
to spend a life crossing again and again the same
hot white driveway. The big digital clock
on the First Bank asks if I'm still here. It's not
a wasted life, I say to no one. I have a lot to show
for it: these rusty nails I picked up by the railroad bridge,
these bricks, these scrubby hills, this mineral blood.

Little Elegy at Bell Cow Creek

With just the summer left before the end
of high school's end, we fastened to a limb
a bit of rope above the small creek bend
and met each day to swing into a swim.

We gave our bodies' weight to frazzled rope,
to swing out past the toothy rocks below,
past death into mid-creek, with only hope
propelling us into the drowsy flow.

All summer long the creaking, frayed rope held.
We dropped in, sank beneath concentric rings
of water, touched the bottom, rose compelled
into our lives to die of other things.

Smith & Sons

The ice chunks stick, a choking in the throat
of aged, withered water pipes and draw plumbers
out on dead cold days. There's a white truck backed
into the gravel drive next door. Across
the side it says in scrawling, confident
red, *Smith & Sons: Most Trusted Name in Plumbing,*
and I remember when the plumber was
just Smith, back when & sons were just two dumb
guys I knew at school, one apt to spend all day
locked in a bathroom stall with a stolen
Playboy. The other's favorite party trick
was slicking up his denim crotch with hairspray
and lighting it on fire to run through
the party crowd singing *Hunka, Hunka, Burning
Love.* Two dogs in a wild pack of strays
that all of us ran in. Still, I don't doubt
the claim the slogan makes. My dumbass friends
have mostly found a way to make themselves
useful. They hammer neatly in the nail
of every blessed year and drink the bourbon
backed with beer of divorces, births, and deaths.
You'll see them pouring salt from paper bags
onto their sidewalks and front steps before
a freeze or sitting in their winter coats
in bleachers at high school basketball games, knees
raised, hands in coat pockets, faces calm and stern.
And though I know it isn't true, I want now
to say they're chieftains, kings, every single one.

What Peter Looked Like Steeping on Water

Maybe like my drunk buddy
trying to ice fish
on a farm pond
in Oklahoma
suddenly ankle deep in cold cow water.

Or like my own small son
staggering across the living room rug
toward his mother.

But maybe like my father,
lifted light
as a bag of popcorn
in my arms,
slippered feet brushing
the floor between the hospice bed
and wheel chair,
voice swallowed in the unmoving ocean
of morphine,
the pupils of his eyes
two little boats
bobbing
somewhere far out
on that motionless sea.

Reunion

In half-darkness, trees breathe like sleeping animals.
A cloud of low wings skims the dim lakescape,

their fluttering obscuring sounds of oars
breaking still water and our aimless chat

about our recklessness in school: rolling
your father's A.T.V. jumping low hills

behind your house; nights driving through the town
a paper cup of Coke and Southern Comfort

between our legs, a .45 stashed
in the glove box; driving blind down dirt roads.

And once upon a yellow hot August noon
you lifted up a piece of scrap sheet metal

from tall late-summer grass to find beneath
a copperhead reared back to strike. You dropped

the metal, sprang a wild jumping dance
a good ten feet backwards, laughed. How are we

alive? And how are we still here, with twenty years
and more behind us, met again to sit

on this flat rock by this small lake,
almost like we were shipwrecked here,

almost like we were the survivors.

Passing

The row of trees that marked the old fence line
was there to give us shelter from the wind.
The knobby oak, rough cedar, and tall pine,
a row of trees to hold the old fence line.
But even oaks will peak and then decline.
We watch the passing of our elder kin,
the row of trees that marked the old fence line
not there to give us shelter from the wind.

III. The Weather at One Horse

After the Grass Fires

My friend Phil, the shuffle-step macabre,
pulls his oxygen tank behind

him on a hand truck. White dogs
come back from sooty fields

a grimmer shade of bone. Phil is thin
in snake-skin boots and walks to the Maverick-mart

for beer (also on the hand truck). Most days
he paints—Mick Jagger in drag, Rocky

and Bullwinkle on roller skates—and eats
dry cereal for dinner again. We watch

the news at 10:00: they show
the interview with a rancher and his son,

how they stood up to their chins
in the dirty farm pond, holding down

the horse while flames scribbled
darkly in the margins. Another word

for human is brown paper and twine.
Yesterday the scrub oak and red cedar

burned like the heart of a saint and the flame-
cleared fields revealed lost tools, arrow heads,

animal bones. Another word for *human*
is—I forget. There is a cement slab

in the burned grass, a bathtub, toilet
and sink in open sunshine. Across

the slab a chimney reaches
like a one-armed man for God. Oh yes,

the word is tinder.

What to Do after a Tornado

Tell them it sounded like a freight train—
they like that—
even if it sounded like your stepfather
taking off his belt, even if it sounded
like the crying baby born in the gym
bathroom during prom. Tell them you never

saw it coming, even if that black wind
had been turning just over your shoulder
since sixth grade. Then excuse yourself

to gather photos scattered through the rubble,
but don't pick up your own. There
are happier families. Look for one of a girl

in blue shorts, aged ten, standing
beside a Ferris wheel with a pink storm cloud
of cotton candy hovering over one hand.
She will be you.

Watch the crows pick through piles
of broken sheetrock and wet carpet.
Throw them what's left of your lucky deck of cards.

When the newspaper man asks you to pose
beside the lone standing closet
where you hid beneath winter coats
and Christmas decorations,
try not to smile for the camera: no one
else should know that you are about
to walk clearly, cleanly, completely
away.

One Horse, Oklahoma, Celebrates the 4th of July

We drive past red plastic cups stuck through chain-link fence
to spell out U.S.A., past lawns full of yard ornaments—
ceramic toadstools, tiny wind mills, a rooster
made from a tractor seat—out to the gravely shoulder
of the highway where firework stands sprout out
from the end of June. When we get home my neighbor
stands in his driveway with his three sons: Gunmetal, Turbine,
and Optimus Prime. Flames are shooting from their hands,
roman candles aimed in mock artillery. The father
drops black cats into his empty beer can, climbs
up his trailer, into the seat of his bass boat to watch
the explosion. Aluminum shrapnel kisses
the lilac bush beside our drive, and I think
of people I know returned from a war I fail
to imagine. They come back with a secret snail curled in the shell
of their eyes, a mystery religion. I feel
like a piece of loose lake-weed bumping the dock. Bullets
of sun bounce off a sky-blue water
tower with the town name tattooed on its forehead. And now
I'm thinking about Cicero, how he said we love
our country most simply because it contains the people
we love. My children get into a little plastic swimming pool. I spray
poison in a liquid jet onto a nest of wasps and watch
the insects drop like drunks. The children are singing patriotic
songs. I am proud to be an American, even
if I don't really know what that means. A pickup
drives by slowly with country music flopping
out the open windows. I belong to this place. Tonight
we will lie upstairs in my daughter's bed
by the window and watch fireworks break overhead like waves
on an invisible beach. In the morning cardboard
tubes of all sizes, the spent casings of firecrackers,
will litter the lawn like the dead at Antietam. Two-a-days
will begin for the high school football team, kids in helmets, shoulder pads,
and gym shorts grunting and running sideways in agility drills. Viewed
from afar, they will be tiny crabs, frantic
for a sea you can't even smell from here.

The Muse

Calliope, when she packed up and came
to Oklahoma, first went out and found
a calico white cotton dress, two out-
side baggy pockets on the front for stuffing tangled
wild onion stocks she gathered from the hills.
She hummed a bit and tried to look less holy.

On Sunday she would belt the hymns with holy-
rollers. They told her they were glad she came.
That's where she met Hank Smith, who lived among the hills
of rusted junk outside of town. They found
a lot to talk about. He liked to comb her tangled
blonde hair and pick the burs and grass bits out.

When folks would ask about her past, her out-
side life, he told them to shove off and holy
shit, now what man could care how tangled
up her dim past might be, when she just came
in from the evening rain, bright as a penny found
inside the pocket of some fresh washed jeans. The hills

bore silent witness of their love, the way the hills
will do. But from his lips the muse called out
a song to make the rusted car parts holy
when morning sun greased down the heaps. He found
himself much lighter since she came,
his thoughts, like clear-burned field, less tangled.

The morning that she found the doe, all tangled
in fencing strung around the rusting hills,
he held her while she cried and later came
to her when tears had wrung her out
and offered up himself to be hers wholly.
And after that entanglement they found

they could not bear to part. The ladies found,
concerned about her absence from the church, them tangled
in knots of naked arms and legs and wholly
unbothered by the knocks that echoed from the hills.
But later on the scrap-man's boy called out
for Hank, and just his weathered hound dog came.

They found him wandering through the hills, his eyes
wrung out: what came from getting tangled up
with all that holy, holy, holy.

Lines Written While Sitting on a Stump

Even we Christians know
it's a serious matter, this carving
up of a living creature.

So, grim behind my safety goggles,
I notch the tree on one face
and make in it a woody, toothless smile

before turning the chainsaw
on its side and slicing though
from the opposite wall of the trunk.

Then the real work begins:
cutting the trunk into sections and splitting
each round with the heavy maul.

Master Chuang says Cook Ting
could carve an ox without
hitting a single bone or sinew,

working the knife like an underwater
ballet. I knew a man who could carve
a tree that way, but today

I am not that man. The chain stays
nervous, jumping often from the bar.
My maul falls too much to one side.

I sweat even in the cool of early November.
I had expected Father Hopkins to meet
me here, after I spent the morning

reading his poems and waiting for sunrise.
I keep trying to recite "The Windhover"
in my head, but you, Li Bai,

what are you doing here
sitting cross-legged between two scrub oaks,
leaves falling on your bald head?

You keep telling me to slow down.
Or stop. You say leave
the wood here and it will split

itself over time. Or, better yet, leave
it long enough under wind and sun
and you won't even have to burn it.

Magic Chicken

There, where lost herds of wild horses chase
the coins of kids around the parking lot,
I brought the bird two offerings, pale coins,
and laid them down inside the silver slot.

The sweet ascending hymn to discount rose
above the bony lines of interred carts
and clucked atop the cloud that stuck above
the giant "M" that tops these discount marts.

This oracle brought truth from painted roost
and laid it where it can't now be denied:
It's us there in the bright translucent egg,
the fragile plastic embryo inside.

The Weather at One Horse

The trunks of sycamores are still as bare
and white as unseen patches of a farmer's
tan, but it's warm enough for wild onions
to tuft a square of grass behind the bail
bonds office just a week after last snow.

When wind starts up again, on flatbed trucks
dogs hunker shivering beside wet loads of hay.

A woman standing on her porch is watching
her husband's truck straddle the mud and ride
the dirty ruts toward town, where he will drink
coffee at the gas station, like every morning since
retiring last month. She knows the cold
still isn't done. She knows what heavy weather
the wind will push in hard after sunset
through lines of scrubby cedar by the road.

Beaver Dam on Bell Cow Creek

The water here is always red
with mud and slides up to the dam
like tongue behind an upper lip.
Cottonmouths stink like something dead;
they hang from scrub oak brush and slip
into the pool above the twiggy jam.

The dam's not more than four feet wide,
not taller than the flat truck tire
half stuck into the muddy bank
and vined with poison oak beside
beer cans, a busted propane tank,
a rusted roll of broken chicken wire.

I never catch the beavers here
but picture them beneath the flow
of runoff, rainwater, mud and piss
and think that if the creek was clear
I'd see them glide through loops and twists,
like glass tank mermaids in a tourist show.

Outside the Downtown Library, OKC

8:00 a.m. and a kid in cowboy boots
sits on the sidewalk smoking
while he talks to the old man
who passes out circulars
for Rent-a-Center.

It's two days before
we remember again the bomb
that leveled a building two blocks
from here, how the front half
collapsed suddenly into dust
like someone who had just walked
a terribly long distance.

Construction workers stand
around this morning with Styrofoam cups
steaming between their hands,
waiting for their weight
to shift toward the day's work.

Then the jackhammer begins
to stutter against concrete like someone
trying to start a prayer.

Flying in After the Ice Storm

Nosing through low and knobby clouds like schools
of humpy fish, descending after winter storms
have glued a skin of glass on everything,
I say a prayer and squint into the shrapnel light.

Then as we land we pass above a street
on which a long, black S.U.V. is turning
sideways on the ice and sliding hard into
the back of the compact hatchback in front of it.
From just above this violence looks a lot
like synchronized ballet. I pray again,
for those below and for us too, up here.
Oh, Lord, let all our swift collisions be
a dance with your headstrong and wild grace.

After the Flood

The faces of the missing continue to float
across the TV news even after the sheetrock

has lifted its skirts two feet off the floor
to show the bare 2x4s beneath.

We have become used to driving around
the stalled cars still abandoned mid-street.

Every night my neighbor puts out a bowl
of food for a dog he hasn't seen in days,

and the possum under his porch
gets fatter. In yards, sidewalks,

and streets, mud puddles gape like open
wounds. The frogs around them sing

with the voices of the drowned while I
stand in the yard with a hair dryer

on an orange extension cord, blowing
through the pages of a book. When night

pours down, those who live closest to the river
can't sleep. They lie in bed and listen

for the sound of whole houses lifted by tongue
of water, straining through the teeth of trees.

The Angels of Juarez

stand on folding
chairs, their feet slippery with sweat
and silver metallic paint.

Behind them a cinder
block wall self-eviscerates
into red, yellow, and green graffiti.

A dry wind chicken-picks goose down
from their wire-framed wings

and tugs at the cardboard
signs that say
assassin repent!
and
corrupt police, look for God!

They are messengers. They are
witnesses. They are evangelical
kids from a little church

on a dirt road. I have never been to Juarez.
What I know about violence is

from the school parking lot,
the time one friend
ripped a guy's ball sack with the tip
of his cowboy boot,

or the time another
cut the earlobe from some punk
outside the all-ages club, the way
the blood fell
in sheets like a woman's
hair.

I've been told that
what my uncle remembered
of Korea
was how the wounded
sat bolt upright

just before
dying.

Another friend says violence
is part of rural life, every girl
and boy knows the flat expression
of a belt.

I want to meet it next time like those angels:
shimmering and completely silent
above the faded flicker of police tape,
wings shading the barefoot orphans ducking in
and out of the scene
of the crime.

Advent

At 4:00 it's getting dark. Thin fog
picks dead leaves from a lone hackberry tree
and drops them on the yellowed grass. Our dog
noses the dead wet leaves and twig debris

and flushes out a burst of quail who try
to break the seal between the earth and sky.

A Funeral Begins at the Church across the Street

Men and women in black, a few at first and then more, move
quickly and silently across the parking lot, like a slow rain
beginning to fall into the dark mouth of the sanctuary.
A blue jay screams curses from the skirts of a pecan tree.

Then comes the small girl the neighbors call
"the urchin," who spends each day alone flitting
around the neighborhood like a trapped moth.
She is surrounded by three patchy dogs.

She marches barefoot and chants a little song
about the summer morning, three stray dogs,
and her very own self. She passes between the mourners,
a blade of blue sky cutting through storm cloud.

When she gets home, her mother will still sit like a sea wall
in front of the Trinity Broadcasting Network with a can of beer.
The urchin will go into the kitchen for a glass of warm tap water.
The man in the coffin will still be dead. The mourners

will still gather and be sad. Nothing will be any better.
The jay will keep screaming its malediction on the deep
down meanness of the world. But, look now, for a moment:
the song, the girl, and three loping dogs.

The Tree Called Mimosa that Blooms Where They Tore the Meth House Down

Pink blossoms like a stripper's tassels strung
among the stringy leaves on slightly bowed,
malnourished limbs make this the tree that suits
our neighborhood. No one has ever sowed

mimosa seeds, not here at least, but still
it thrives, like us, because it lacks the sense
not to: our greenish flag, our blooming sign,
our scraggly self against the chain-link fence.

Spring Comes to One Horse, Oklahoma

Winter slinks away, leaving mailboxes
leaning each way on rotting posts,
gathered along the street, stunned like dead
on the day of resurrection. We rise
a little earlier, even on Saturday,
and sit in plastic lawn chairs to feel
wind shifting north, south, north,
like a boy walking back and forth
in front of the house where a girl lives.

Everywhere the smell of coffee
in Styrofoam cups, bacon frying.
Overhead, the spry agitation of squirrels
shaking the first nervous blooms of redbud.

Everyone's lawn needs mowing.
Everyone's windows are open.
And, one by one, the men are crawling
beneath cars and trucks on cement blocks
and metal ramps. Wrenches in hand, they know,
against all flat good sense, that this year
they can make those engines run.

IV. Ambition

Ambition

My missing student turns Poseidon
through tattooed knuckles during office hours,
fidgeting with a piece from the chess set
I bought in Athens twenty years ago,
the set that's sold in every tourist shop,
with gods for pieces on a marble board.
He's telling how he spent the last three weeks
away from class riding his wild moods
like he's a hero in a silent film
lashed to a fresh chopped log and rushing down
a mountain millstream toward a chewing blade.
He says he's on the stuff again. "The stuff"
is what he says, and I don't ask what stuff.
I look more at the clock that hangs behind
his head like some medieval painted halo
than at his eyes. He's missed three weeks
of Shakespeare, but he says he wants to be
"the next Will Shakespeare," says he wants "so bad
to be a great." And I am staring now
at a small pile of rejection slips
beside their torn envelopes on my desk,
right next to three large stacks of freshman papers
I have to grade before I leave today.
What does he want from me? He says he can
get straight. He's got a girlfriend and a kid
he wants to be a family with but thinks,
too, that he's got to suffer for his art,
that all that Berryman, Van Gogh, and Bird
jazz about dying all the time to live
your art is true. He's put Poseidon down
and taken up Apollo now. I think
about a night in Delphi, New Year's Eve,
when college friends and I sneaked from the club
our tour group partied at and walked beneath
the stone-faced moon to the Castalian Spring
at Mt. Parnassus by the highway side,
sacred, our guide had said, to poets and their muse.
It was a little bulge of rock that spoke
an arc of water through the air
into a pool squared in wet stone a foot
or two below. Castalia was another nymph

the god Apollo chased into the form
we know her in. We drank and risked who knows
what sort of pain, intestinal and otherwise,
then went into our lives to make our names.

And here I am. I've changed my great ambition
from being well remembered to forgetting
a little less of what I read. I tell
the student all the things he's got
are things that Shakespeare writes about. I mean
the love, the loss, the trying just to make
the human life you've got work out. You are
such stuff as plays are made on, even if
unknowing puts parentheses around us all.
We want so much to tell the story, we
forget that we ourselves make up the tale.

But then my office hours end,
and ruckus from a Frisbee game begins
on campus green beneath the window.
I rise to shake his blue-inked hand and say
stick with the class, stay off the stuff, and try
to turn the paper in. He says nothing
but nods before he walks away. Outside
the game goes on and someone laughs
a light ascending laugh that flitters up
to perch behind me on the sunlit window ledge.

The Professor Pauses Mid-Lecture

Each word's a pickled egg, the lecture
a grimy jar. Outside everything
blooms funky and hot
like landscape done by Prince
                  (the sun hands out yellow lollipops)
and students keep their eyes

crawling like houseflies on the window glass.
By one and two they start to nod and startle,
nod and startle until
the whole backrow looks like a horn section
grooving in sync. The clock, too, falls asleep
and slides off the wall.

My lectern slits its wrists and falls—I have to go
impromptu. But look! One student taking notes!
A miniscule, curling script
that when I'm close enough to see turns out
to be tiny doodled birds: a thousand gray flitting swallows
in swirling liftoff. Even I bid her fly.

Down the Throat of Drought

Drawn to the window by a sound like rain
beginning drop by drop to slowly fall,

I find only the plock of grasshoppers
thumping the vinyl siding. There's a crowd

of browned hibiscus nodding in parched wind
dumbly. I've been a long time dry,

and my rebar is starting to show.
I'm looking at a long tin shed

across the road, its roof sagged like a worn-
down mule. Three empty cans of Miller Lite

are floating in the Queen Anne's lace that lines
the drainage ditch, and, down the road,

the balding veterinarian walks through
the double doors out of his clinic to smoke

beside the mailbox in his violet scrubs.
It's almost noon. The sun's been dragged halfway

across the sky like an old stump pulled
from its socket with chains. Cars move through thin

hot light and disappear in shimmers.
All morning long a friend who's dead has been

rising closer to the surface of my mind,
the way a splinter left will work its own

slow way out from the flesh.

Works and Days

Snow shuffled with rain,
makes New York a puddle
of slush as I leave the famous café

where I read my poems
to ten people in a dim basement.
I could not distinguish their applause

from the clank of dinnerware upstairs.
I'm standing at Canal and something,
my book of poems tucked like a fish wrapped in paper

under my arm, so I can keep my hands warm
in tweedy pockets, and I'm thinking
about my father who used to walk

through the streets of the East Village
in the sixties with a guitar he couldn't play
slung over his shoulder by the neck

like a fence post his own daddy may have carried
to the edge of the tiny farm in Oklahoma.
What do any of us know about work?

We look for it. We find it. We hate it or love it.
We give our bodies to it wholly, like the air of a place.
Three workers in coveralls are unloading a truck

by the midnight curb, boxes sliding down a metal ramp
out the back, pushed down the rollers by one man,
received at the bottom by another and then passed

to the third who stacks them on a hand-truck.
I watch them for a few stretched minutes, my shoes
getting wetter in the snow. I am delaying

my ride up the elevator to the little hotel room
in China Town, where I will open the curtains to look
down on the street below, watch the water freezing

in the gutter, listen hard as it silently
slides over the ice beneath.

Berryman

I wake up with you standing on my brain
again, the rain's small words on window slurred.
It's cold. I think my pillow smells like chain-

smoking. But I don't smoke. Not at all absurd
that you should be lashing my brain just now;
I fell asleep beside your book & heard

you sawing on my dreams all night, like how
magicians cut up ladies they have lured
into their boxes on the stage, then—wow!—

they're whole again. You say you want a word
re: Jason of the golden fleece, the vow
he broke, the broken children he interred,

& how, his love and fame all gone, you saw
his body swinging from the Argo's bow.

Squirrel

As nervous as the corner hustle man,
he clambers up the wooden fence out back
to chide some subtle slight in the deadpan
faces the nodding-off hydrangeas make.

So, this is how the squirrel unspools the thread
of one whole summer afternoon. Just see
the way he grows a bramble in his head
and hugs a fire to his heart, like me.

Wedding Dress in a Thrift Shop Window

Skull white its little beaded flowers on
a white background, it hangs among the *bric-
a-brac*: a pair of old snowshoes, a thick
rug of imitation Persian weave, a lawn
flamingo with a missing leg. The pawn
shop wouldn't take it, but they couldn't stick
it in the trash, I guess. So now its slick,
satiny sides grow pale in windowed sun.

Was it left here before the bouquets wilted,
or was it kept for many years in glory
before its owner died? I think they size it
rarely, the newly blooming brides, and, jilted
completely now, it's pure *memento mori,*
a paper skull—unless somebody buys it.

Free Pianos

The bulky uprights bunched like foreheads, hunched
as buffalo, and lined up as in mug-
shots in the weekly freebie papers: scrunched
in family room corners, squared like a shrug.
And baby grands unsteady on thin legs,
their tops propped open like a surgeon's work.
Or low consoles topped with framed photo dregs
of decades past, the keys less smile than smirk.
All free to anyone with means to haul
them off in hunkered trucks, or better still,
in trailers tugged behind the car, with all
the benches placed legs-up like stiff roadkill.
Hauled off, they hit each bump with groaning tones
that sound a bit like my own untuned bones.

The Road to Damascus

The trees had stretched themselves and taken off
their thick, grey coats of empty winter sky.

The birds were chanting fifty holy names.
But I was listening only to the passing

plane overhead and to the grousing sound
of traffic. Sitting in the little park

I pressed my hands against the earth behind
me, felt a humming that could be the tune

your name is sung to. But I didn't hear.
You chased me as a spark runs down a fuse.

When winter came again, I found a note
in my coat pocket. It said exactly this:

Someone you meet along the road who throws
you to your knees and shines you blind, you know

him always after that, the way you know
a friend's voice on the phone. Man in a cave,

stop scratching at the walls. Be still. Listen
and you will hear him breathing in the dark.

Bonhoeffer at the Abyssinian Baptist Church

If all that rises praises you, my Lord,
then bodies sprung from pews can picture forth
saints springing up in bloom from stony earth.
The hands that higher rise and halo toward
the pendant lights catch a gleam and clap
as if a choir of holy beings praises,
descending but to bring us up, and raises
us all until the binding cords go snap.
But you, that love me, tell me to go back?
To grasp the cord and haul myself toward ground,
down, to the home that everywhere I lack.
So, tell me now, how can a way be found
to sing your praises in my fatherland,
that foreign land?

Possum

On feet bare like a desert saint's, it pads
across the porch and toward the dry cat food
my wife pours out for strays. It doesn't scare
when I stomp, bellow, toss a pebble
at its rump, just hisses at me, geezerly,
and keeps on chewing. Eyes like little radio
dials and fur like coal snow, smog sky, or anything
smudged, dirty, it reminds me of the boy
in school we called Possum for how he slept
through class and how his eyes were beaded black,
his nose sharpened to needle fine. When at last
I knock it off the porch with one quick blow
from a snow shovel, it scuttles under
a shrub and disappears into the house's
cracked stone foundation, knowing more than I—
beneath the sound of footfall, chair-scrape, voice
descending like the ash of distant fire—
the saint's strange way to practice death.

Ignatius' Letter to the Romans

Be silent. Hush. Take up the sound of ooze
like oil from olives that the presses bruise.
Or be the sound of fresh baked loaves, the sound
of seeds beneath the stony, sun-packed ground.
I'll be the noise of wheat beneath the stone,
or, caught jammed in the leopard's throat, a bone
rattling jagged, heard as just a wheeze
the beast exhales into the copper breeze.
Or hush and let the leopard's windpipe be
a tunnel I stumble through as best I can
in darkness which obscures but can't consume,
from which I'll come into the sun to see
the full-sized shadow of a full-grown man
thrown on the grass beside the empty tomb.

After a Vision of Christ, Peter Goes to be Crucified

As I slipped from Jerusalem I met
a man who limped along the stony road:
the crucified not cross-afflicted yet,
although the cross had hung his fleshy load.
The priest had torn his perfumed robe and cried
that I must die, or so I had been told.
So, as another clammy dawn was pried
out of the sheep-loud hills, I met the cold
and left. Then as I walked along, I eyed
the road ahead until at last it showed
to me this man who walked my way. He spied
me; I spied Him. And passing by I slowed
to ask his path. He said, "To death once more."
So I turned back the heavy way that I had walked before.

View of Scheveningen Sands by Hendrick Van Anthonissen after Restoration Reveals a Beached Whale

The restorer's scalpel first reveals a man
standing midair and then the whale he stands
on like a fallen monolith in windy
shallows off the beach of Scheveningen Sands.

Emaciated ships thrown further up
the strand suggest a storm has beached the whale,
but now blue sky begins to spread above
gray sand where salvage carts have scored their trail.

Though changing notions of good taste explain
what moved some hand unknown to thin the whale
until it blended with gray sea and sky,
one stretch of empty ocean wetly pale,

it's much less clear what all those people bunched
for years in tufts like grass across the beach
until now thought that they were gathered there to view,
Leviathan unseen within their reach.

Works and Days #2

In the all-night grocery, making angels
by staring at the pendant lights
then squeezing my eyes shut, I wait

behind my register for the drunks
and assortedly medicated to bring
their Fritos, their Cheetos, their Busch

and Bud (two beers so many years at war
in my youth, like Iran and Iraq).
At 2:00 a.m. I sell a pack of milk duds,

some cigarettes and a bloody rack
of ribs. The other two cashiers
take their break together and go

out to the parking lot to practice
the wrestling moves they have been discussing
over empty lanes for hours, while I compose

songs about how I am wasting
my life to piped in tunes by Elton John
and Journey. Somewhere in the long tube

of night I start thinking about a dream
I had once, asleep on a couch in Tulsa,
about a great brown bear

in a cage. I knew the grizzly
was my soul, felt it separate
from each cell in my body, a buzzing

like pulling a living bee apart by tugging
on the wings, and woke knowing
what it feels like to die.

Deep in the supra-lighted
bowels of the supermarket, a lean old man
in meats leans toward a glass case

to stare at the dead fish as if they might move, as if this were a living aquarium.

Alley Cat

High-stepping through the melting snow, it walked
into our yard then hunkered low and stalked
a splash of cardinal red in all that white.
With every string inside the cat pulled tight,
time stopped. Behind the foggy window I observed
the cat that hunts the bird and has a bird
fluttering inside its chest, and thought it's time I start
to hunt and still my own deceiving heart.

Waking New Year's Day

I'm peeled from sleep by sound from a gas flare
off an oil well, something like a train

run up a gravel bank, and can picture
the tongue of flame licking

at salt gray sky. West
of here revelers are just arriving

home, carrying their shoes
through their own quiet

houses. Outside this window, patchy
snow and the white faces of Herefords

damp with fog, their chewing
the only visible movement.

This year I will cross the little stream
into my fourth decade. It's getting so

even a good hunter would know my passing
only by a few broken twigs.

The Haircut

In rubber boots
and running shorts, I lean

over the rail
of our back deck and buzz

my head. A stray
cat licks its stretched toes clean

then lifts its paw
to swat at drifting fuzz.

The shaver coughs
and rattles in my ears,

mixed with the noise
my kids make while they play.

And when there's only
stubble left, the shears

shut off. I watch
the fresh-cut tufts of gray

blow loose, float free
like little boats set out to sea.

V. The Field of Fathers

Dad Band

Because we're going to die we bang out Joy
Division covers in the hot garage.
Convulsing pegboard wrenches, we destroy
a quiet afternoon beneath a gnarled barrage
of songs we've hauled like marlins from the deep
green sea of distant youth. A sweet guitar
in sunburst orange or slinky black is cheap
compared to payments on a new sports car,
so midway on the mosey through our lives
my oldest friend arrives with his snare drum
held like a dish of casserole. Our wives
retreat into the house. Our kids don't come.
Cranking the amps, we ride the squeal and fuzz
back to a glorious youth that never was.

The Family Vacation

A landlocked family at the beach, the sea
of grass behind us traded for the actual sea,
we stare into the glaring blue, the sea
touched with eternity like Sunday afternoons.

Each morning I witness our children wade
into the endless deep, then afternoons
of Skee-Ball in the beach arcade, rolling
the wooden ball into the neon lights.

The kids aren't little anymore, teen-aged
or nearly. Gone are floaties for their arms
and duckie rings around their waists, but still
I watch them like I am the last lighthouse

and they are little wooden ships with sails
of silken child's hair. My father walked
the bottom of the creek from side to side
before he'd let us jump from the raised bank.

I cannot walk the ocean floor. I have
to trust the ocean with my kids but stay
nearby and glance from one to one to one,
like counting birds and always losing count.

At sundown I am fully spent. The sea
pants like a softly sleeping animal
Curled in its cave of night. And then I dream
my long passed grandmother up from the sea

of grass she sleeps beneath. She's come to tell
me something, but her words are just the sound
of waves against the washing sand until
I start to hear the voice inside the surf:

They wade into the light, she says. Each thing
that dies. The songs and poems, women and men,
the boys and girls, the towns, the books, the thoughts.
It all goes down into the blessed light.

When morning washes up, pale gray and wet
before the heat burns in, we hit the beach
again. This time I stay a little closer
still, but still the words inside the surf.

The sea of grass, the sea of blazing water,
the sea of light. We all go in. We all
go under. And the children that I watch
turn slowly in the surf to watch me back.

Toward November

The cold comes in riding bareback
on a wild wind. It's a man
with close-cropped hair who tells us
all about how he's "a real straight shooter." My father

was born in February. In a few months
I'll sit in a bar he never visited
and raise a glass. Today my children
are picking over the lawn beneath
the pecan trees, looking for nuts
they will sell the co-op for 10 cents a pound,
their fingers trailing through stunted
grass for what the wind whipped loose.

There is really so little I can do to protect them.

Tonight I will take my bald spot for a walk
beneath a horde of stars in pointy hats
and pause beneath the nearly empty
office building to look up
into an eighth-floor pane of glass
where my heart sits at a metal desk
going over the numbers, going over
the numbers again.

Neglect

An orange-brown halo on the slab outside
  beside the cooling unit's bulk, a soil
    and blood smudged ring of rust around the pair
of needle-nosed pliers with which I tried
  to fix a leaking air conditioning coil.
    I left the thing unfixed. It got too cool to care.

The pliers are now flecked with the same turn
  to orange that's drained the trees of their green oil,
    they're both alight to show the year's unblinking stare,
aflame to show us how all things will burn
        in air.

The Better David

My son brings home a paper David made
in Bible school, a crayoned cut-out, the swirl
of whistling sling above his head. "He obeyed
our God," he says. *Until he saw a girl,*
I finish in my head, thinking of pale
moonlight, pale bare limbs seen from high up,
a soldier dead, the prophet's sad shepherd's tale,
a baby waning like a wafer in a cup.
But soon enough he'll feel the flimsy stuff
from which his heroes all are made. No need
for me to point it out to him, this rough
life's truth. Instead I'll offer book and creed,
confess that I, a paper David too,
must let the greater David do what I can't do.

Praying for Dogs

A tumor like a portabella on its neck,
a Pomeranian has poked its head
into my timeline where its owner posts
please pray. And later at the Wednesday night
prayer meeting Widow Jones requests a word
of intercession for her labradoodle
who has a blockage in his doggy gut
and is as bloated as a bullfrog's chin.
And so at night I find myself in prayer
like this: *O, Lord of endless mercy, Lord*
of grace and wonder, please bring healing down
to Cupcake and to Captain Fluffyface.

The list grows by the day. My buddy texts
to ask for prayer when his great Dane gets hit
by a school bus. My kids come home from sleep-
overs and ask their mom and me to pray
for all the dogs of friends: the overweight
and cancerous dachshund, the beagle plagued
with heartworm, three asthmatic pugs who snort
and cough like dirt-clogged carburetors.

So without ceasing now I pray for them.
O, Father God, I lift up Bruno, Dot,
and Buster. God, I pray for Stinky Pete.
O, You who made the endless cosmos run,
who hung the stars and filled the ocean depths,
who brought your people out of Egypt's yoke
and raised our savior from the dead, please bless
Little Lord Fartington.

                   What else am I
to do? They mean so much to all those who
grind open cans of wet and stinking meat
to drop into their doggy bowls, who clean
up all the splendid messes that they make
by eating pillows and crapping feather tufts
on kitchen floors, who brush the beggar's lice
and tangles from their ever-shedding coats.

To pray for one dog is to pray for all
of us. And so, I bow my head again,
scoop up the scattered kibbles and loose bits,
and kneel beside the sloppy water dish.

Croquet

English game with a French name,
beloved of Scots-Irish Okies,
played on lawns that were little

more than weeds mowed low. Across south-
eastern Oklahoma, after church,
at every family gathering, out came

the rack of wooden balls and mallets,
the double-diamond pattern of white
wire wickets pushed into hard dirt.

My grandfather would hurry from his shed,
printer's ink streaking his fingers,
to grip the mallet and dangle it

like the clapper of a bell between his legs.
(Was it as nakedly masculine as that?)
The men in my family who printed

newspapers, husked corn, painted houses, burned
in refineries, took this game of English
aristocracy as seriously as Monday night

football, delighted in knocking their opponents' balls
(It was as masculine at that) across the road
into the dandelion scruff and poison

oak that swarmed the drainage ditch. Children
were granted no mercy, knocked aside and left
to tap the painted stake long after the men

had adjourned to fried chicken and cans of beer,
having driven their balls over grass and dirt clods
in lines as wobbly and erratic as their table talk.

I think about these men sometimes when playing
whiffle ball with my kids in the backyard, gripping
a plastic bat as big and red as the nose

of a cartoon drunk, swinging three inches above
each pitch to let my five-year-old son
strike me out, throwing the game

even when the kids start to trash talk: *Daddy, you stink
like a diaper.* I want to build them up
more than I want to win.

But every now and then, I hunker into my serious stance,
eye the ball for real, and knock one over
the privacy fence and into the alley

behind our house. Then I hear those men, who
had to take any victory they could—
even from their own children—

clapping their calloused hands as I round the little plastic bases.

The Day Begins

The living frighten all the resting dead
in Syria where a young man has crawled

into an ancient burial cave to hide
his family from the screaming shells at night.

And at the breakfast table I chew out
my son who tipped his glass of chocolate milk

across white tablecloth. All day I'll feel
guilty for it. And in the drop-off line

at school the parents creep forward in cars,
one eye fixed on the tiny screens they hold,

until a Lexus crunches the backside
of a white S.U.V in front of it,

the driver getting out to yell at her
reflection in the tinted driver's window.

In Syria the bombs and bones of all
the ancient dead are like parentheses

around the man and his five crying kids.
If we are drowning here, it's just because

we're sitting down in shallow water.

The Way to Cumae

Well into winter wasps drunkenly bang
their heads against sun-backed windows. We find
them, one or two, fretting the glass and know
there is a swarm somewhere inside the walls.
One day my daughter brings a note from school,
not pinned like a corsage, just folded primly
in three and slipped into an envelope.
It says some kids at school have been writing
obscenities in excrement on bathroom walls.
It says the bathrooms will be monitored
and this is to inform us and to make
us all aware. I am aware.

                      Here is
another little worry to be dropped
into the bucket full of rocks I lug
around all day. One to replace the wasps,
this thinking of the children like my girl—
who last night lined a dozen stuffed cats up
and made me come to see the fur parade—
smearing anger and waste on cinderblock
walls where my daughter tinkles.

                        Nothing
in books with which I've lined my feeble brain
prepared me for this stuff: not Shakespeare, who
has much to say about daughters, and not
Sam Beckett who has much to say about
excrement. I'm scrambling like a flightless wasp
gone mad to make its way up slick, cold glass.

The last time I sat down with my father,
we looked out into fields where cattle mulled
in settling evening light. A tractor thumped
nearby. He asked me what I have been reading
and if I've kept my oil changed. In two
more months he was dissolving like a pinch
of sugar on his hospice bed.

                     Sometimes
I dream about the game I played those nights

of high school boredom: turning off headlights
to see how far I dared to drive through dark.
Sometimes I pull and pull the switch, but the lights
won't come back on.

                    There's one thing that I read:
how Virgil is surprisingly clear on
the entrance to the underworld. He says
it's near Averna's sulfurous shore in Cumae,
the Sibyl's cave. So, that's the way one goes
to talk with fathers who are dead.

Sonnet in which I Apologize by Comparing our Marriage to a Truck

That time I slammed the back French doors then kicked
that concrete planter off the deck and broke
my toe, the neighbors saw the whole conflict,
one-sided no doubt, and I was the joke
around the block for weeks, until the Kent
kid took a dump in their front yard. What I
in all my rage and slobber meant
is that I love you. Something's wrong with my
temp gauge and radiator, which always
blows up just when the truck gets going. So
I put us up on blocks to sit for days
until you get the parts to make us go
again. The hood is gone. I've stripped the gears.
But we can make this engine run for years.

Sonnet in Which I Apologize for Comparing our Marriage to a Truck

We'll make this engine run for years, I say,
as if it ran on diesel, but we will
go on much better if I put away
the strained quatrains and try to be more real.
I know it's not the greatest metaphor
to summarize the sacrament of love.
Loose ends—like what, for instance, is the door?
Or what is symbolized by the loose glove
box that falls open every time we hit
a bump?—undo the knot that ties the tenor
to vehicle (or, so to speak). I'll quit
stretching this lame conceit from thin to thinner,
and focus more on being here right now:
real presence better drives our wedding vow.

Grown-Ass Man

A man backs a tractor slowly down metal ramps
behind a flatbed truck and begins to mow
the empty lot across the street at 5:30
on a summer Monday morning.

I am standing on the front porch drinking coffee
before I drive my mother to chemo. I watch
the tractor drag its large, flat mower
around the lot, listen to the pings of rock

bouncing up against metal deck.
Last fall, they tore down the house
that used to be there, its peeling roof patched
only by leaves fallen from one large oak.

There were stacks of car batteries by the front door,
and for three months an abandoned baby
doll with one missing eye sat
on the roof outside the attic window.

Now, stirred from tall grass by the mower,
a white dog noses an empty can of energy
drink by the curb, lifts its leg and lowers
it again without pissing. I am 39 this week.

I am learning to walk slowly beside
my small son when we go to the library
down the street. I am learning to walk
slowly beside my mother into the cancer clinic.

As the mower powers down, I hear
my neighbor's voice suddenly loud
in argument with his wife. *I am
a grown-ass man,* he is yelling.

I am a grown-ass man, he repeats,
and I repeat it too, quietly,
liking the sound of it.

Field

Heaven is a field I am
driving an old truck across
in the only dream I have
on the subject. The sky over
that pasture is so blue I know
it will burst if it doesn't turn
twenty different reds
at evening. The truck
is my granddad's '72 Ford, still smelling
of oilfield and aftershave. When it stalls
I get out and lift the hood but look
instead into the everlasting distance
dotted with cattle and streaked
with blotches where the henbit
has bruised the pasture purple.
I think of my father lifting
me onto his lap to let
me drive as we bumped over clumps
of gopher dirt in the pasture,
how I steered
wildly through the grass
his boot barely on the gas.
But it is my father
in law who is standing
next to me when I look,
who has bloodied his knuckles
starting the engine
running again, who is gesturing
with a patience he rarely had
in life for me to get back
into the truck and drive on.

I wake to hear our children breathe their sleep
one room over, and to tell you, love
of all my lifetime, as we lie beneath
our ceiling in the middle
of our bed, in the middle
of our life, that heaven
has a field full
of fathers. I have been
there. I am one of them.

www.ingramcontent.com/pod-product-compliance
Lightning Source LLC
Chambersburg PA
CBHW030846090426
42737CB00009B/1124